The Triplets

A Bizarre Comedy

by John Reason

WWW.SAMUELFRENCH.CO.UK
WWW.SAMUELFRENCH.COM

FOR AMATEUR PRODUCTION ENQUIRIES

UNITED KINGDOM AND WORLD EXCLUDING NORTH AMERICA

plays@SamuelFrench-London.co.uk

020 7255 4302/01

Each title is subject to availability from Samuel French, depending upon country of performance.

THE TRIPLETS

An anteroom in the Town Hall of a large town. There is a conference table and chairs to one side. A trestle table with a white cloth is set for a buffet.

The time is the present. The room is decorated with streamers, and a banner from wall to wall reads: 'Happy Birthday to our Triplets – 18-- to 19--.'

At the start, PAULINE, ROBERTA and HAM are on stage. As the banner proclaims, they are 100 years old. They are also triplets. They do not look alike. They are, however, dressed alike in black leotards and white pumps - overlaid with 'Little Girl' flowered frocks and matching ribbons. HAM wears a mask and wig indicative of a beauty queen.

They are standing, in isolation, in different parts of the stage.

A long silence.
Nothing occurs.
Then PAULINE starts to snivel.
ROBERTA looks at her.
PAULINE stops.
Then HAM moves to the conference table and attempts to clamber on to it. She scrabbles across the top of table, her legs kicking. She stops, half on, half off. She breathes in and out deeply and noisily.
ROBERTA looks at her.
HAM stops 'breathing'.
Pause.

ROBERTA   (suddenly) I'm going to have a vol-au-vent.

                             (She moves to buffet. Selects a vol-au-vent,
                             turns to PAULINE.)

                             Want one?

                             (PAULINE shakes her head. ROBERTA bites
                             into pastry. Swallows. Smacks her lips.)

                             Nice. This sort of thing isn't your style is it,
                             Pauline dear? Delicacies. Airy, light ...this
                             style isn't your thing.

                             (She eats. PAULINE snivels. ROBERTA looks
                             at her. PAULINE stops.)

                             I shouldn't cry, dear. Don't cry.

                             (A weak effort from HAM once more. She
                             groans. ROBERTA moves to her.)

                             Ham. You won't make it. Get down. You'll
                             disintegrate. You're one hundred years old;
                             you'll fall apart. (pause)   You'll rupture some-
                             thing vital. You're not as young as you used to
                             be. (ROBERTA moves away. Stares up at
                             banner.)   Come here, Pauline. Come and see
                             how much we're loved. Look what they've done
                             for us. I feel very proud. I could sing.

                             (She hums an age-old tune, but runs out of breath.
                             She sits in a chair.
                             PAULINE moves down to her.)

PAULINE   Roberta ....?

ROBERTA   Yes, dear .....what a lovely old song that is ...

PAULINE   I'm frightened....

ROBERTA   Mother used to sing that song, remember?

PAULINE   I want to go home. That's all I want to do.

ROBERTA   What a lovely old song that is ....

               (Pause. PAULINE starts to snivel.)

               Oh, Pauline, do stop it, Have a vol-au-vent.
               Do stop it; you'll dehydrate yourself. You won't
               look pretty if you cry. We mustn't let Ham take
               all the attention. By the way, dear, tell her to
               get off the table; it's newly polished, I swear.
               She takes no notice of me. I think she's forgotten
               me. Not surprising, I suppose. We all live so
               far away from each other.... we don't get to
               see each other at all. I don't think I've seen
               Ham since eighteen ninety-two. (calling) Ham,
               do get off that table. It's not yours. You'll
               scratch it. (to PAULINE) Now, what were you
               saying my dear?.... oh yes, it is a lovely old
               song. You're so right. (Pause. ROBERTA
               sways and hums for a moment.) God is always
               at Ascot. He sits in the enclosure.

               (Pats PAULINE's hand. Whispers.)

               He doesn't bet, though. Oh no.

PAULINE   (determined) I'm going home, Roberta ....
               (Starts for door.)

ROBERTA   Don't be silly. How far do you think you'll get,
               dressed like that? You'll be raped. You'll be
               ravished. Oh, the world's so wicked. Do come
               and sit down, my dear. You must wait for the
               Queen. The Queen's coming in a very little
               while. (desperately) Look what they've done
               for us.

               (Pause. PAULINE sits in chair.
               HAM starts to scramble again.
               The other two watch her.
               With grunts and wheezes, HAM, in the most

ungainly way imaginable, hauls herself on to the
table-top with one final effort. She lies spread-
eagled on it - motionless.
Pause.)

Well, that's that. Now Ham can have a little sleep.
She's had to travel a long way, of course.
Yarmouth. That's right the other side of London.
A terrible long way. I'm all right at Windsor. It's
no distance at all these days. And God drives the
train. He always does that. (pause) I think I'll
snatch another vol-au-vent. (She gets up and
goes to buffet. Selecting:) No. No, I'll have a
canapé. (Takes one. Swallows.) Delightful.
Do have one, Pauline.

(PAULINE shakes her head.)

You are silly. (playfully) Silly Pauline.

(PAULINE doesn't respond. ROBERTA moves
round touching the streamers.)

Our old town. All this. So kind. (pause) We
mustn't appear ungrateful. That would never do.

PAULINE	I'm not ungrateful.
ROBERTA	Of course you're not.
PAULINE	I'm not.
ROBERTA	No, no, no....
PAULINE	I'm just .... frightened. (pause) He touched my pianos.
	(Pause.)
ROBERTA	Pardon?
PAULINE	The councillor. He came to see me Friday night.

..... a councillor .....

ROBERTA   Yes, it was a councillor who came for me too.
               Very nice man. I offered him a sherry. He
               declined, of course.

PAULINE   He put his fingers all over my pianos. I've got
               four pianos in the parlour I have, and I've got
               two in the kitchen and three in the bedroom ...
               he looked at them. The councillor looked at
               them. He touched them.

ROBERTA   Did he? Mine wasn't like that. Mine didn't
               touch anything. He was a gentleman.

PAULINE   What did he expect, Roberta....?

ROBERTA   One never knows with the opposite sex. I've
               had three husbands and I never knew what they
               expected.

PAULINE   He put his hands all over my pianos then asked
               me if I was musical.

ROBERTA   Mine demonstrated all the proprieties, I will
               say that. He told me I didn't look a day over
               ninety-five.

PAULINE   I told him, no. No, I'm not musical. I just
               can't afford furniture. (pause) Then he showed
               me this dress and these ribbons.

ROBERTA   Mine did that too. He asked me to try them on...

PAULINE   Asked me to try them on....

ROBERTA   To see how they fitted....

PAULINE   See how they fit ...

               (Pause.)

ROBERTA   Did yours help you on with anything?.... or
                   help you off with anything....?

PAULINE   Oh, no, I wouldn't allow anything like that.

                   (Pause.)

ROBERTA   (too quickly) Nor me, nor me....

PAULINE   Much later, he sat me in the back of a motor-
                   car....

ROBERTA   The back? The back?

PAULINE   He wanted to break me in. I was frightened,
                   you see. He wanted to break me in for the short
                   drive.

ROBERTA   I sat at the front. Right at the front.

PAULINE   I sat at the back.

                   (Pause.)

ROBERTA   I sat next to the driver, next to the councillor.
                   He offered to break me in too. 'Get away with
                   you,' I said. 'There's nothing new to me under
                   the sun.' (Laughs.) He seemed very amused at
                   that. Quite diverted. When I think of it, he
                   reminded me of Jamie. Jamie was my second.
                   He had the same shaped thighs as Jamie.

                   (Pause.)

PAULINE   I think they'll take my pianos away from me ...

ROBERTA   Surely not.

PAULINE   It's taken me all my life to get hold of them...

ROBERTA   Why should they want your pianos, Pauline?
                   Men of that calibre are not hard up for the odd

instrument.

PAULINE   I've worked and slaved for them. Other people
           buy sideboards and dressers and bureaux ....

ROBERTA   I've got an antique tall-boy ....

PAULINE   But my pianos mean more to me than all the tea
           in Israel.

ROBERTA   I understand that, my dear. I feel much the
           same about my tall-boy. I wouldn't part with
           that for all the Jews in China.

PAULINE   I feel so helpless, Roberta. Everything I've
           ever loved has been taken away from me. The
           older I get, the more is taken .... last week -
           last week, the gasman turned me off.

ROBERTA   Did he?

PAULINE   The gasman turned me off. I couldn't cook so
           much as a lettuce.

ROBERTA   How abysmal.

PAULINE   I've got no money. I told him I'd got no money.
           'I've got no money,' I said.

ROBERTA   How abysmal.

PAULINE   I'll die of cold. I'll starve. I'm an old woman.
           I can't leap over fences like I used to. I asked
           him to have pity.

ROBERTA   There's plenty of that to go round, I've always
           found.

PAULINE   He'd used it all up. He hadn't got two bits of pity
           to rub together. 'I haven't got two bits of pity
           to rub together,' he said.

ROBERTA

How strange. I've always found my gasman most accommodating.

PAULINE

The gas board is trying to kill me.

ROBERTA

I wonder. I've always thought it had a big heart. Very big-hearted. As big as a gasometer. (Titters.)

PAULINE

(sobbing) I'm frightened....

(She sobs on - quietly. ROBERTA's attention is arrested by HAM,who stirs on the tabl e. She raises herself on to her hands and knees. Finally, she stands upright. She walks to the U.S. end of the table, turns, and poses to the audience like a beauty queen. Then she strolls down the length of the table, hips swinging; turns,looks back over her shoulder, Marilyn Monroe-fashion,then walks back up the table. Faces front.Poses once more. When she speaks, it is with a piping voice. Her half of an interview.)

HAM

Knocks yer eyes out, doesn't it?I'm Hanna from the South of England. I won my final easily. Oh yes. Yes, I have a lot of hobbies. Well, I like killing mayflies. Yes, it might seem a strange hobby to you - but it's seasonal. I like anything seasonal. (She swings her hips.) Knocks yer eyes out, doesn't it? What else? Well, when I've finished with mayflies - round about April - I start on earwigs and butterflies. I really go to town. Oh yes, it is a constructive hobby. I really go to town. You can see me out in the countryside any day - stamping and swatting. I really go to town. My favourite food is peanut butter. That's right, and my big ambition is to live to be a hundred. Yes, I am quite a dish, aren't I? Give me a big hand. Yes, give me a nice big hand. Come on now ... (She walks the table again. She then falters, puts her hand to her chest, breathing deeply.)

ROBERTA   Do be careful, Ham. You'll fall.

                (HAM still talks to an imaginary interviewer.)

HAM   Sorry about that. I get short of breath around
                the lung region. Yes, I'll travel the world.

ROBERTA   Get down - please.

HAM   I won't spend all the prize money at once, no.
                But I'll travel the world.

ROBERTA   Ham.

HAM   New York? Yes, I'd like to see New York. And
                Paris. Mmm.

ROBERTA   You'll scratch the table, dear.

HAM   Well yes, as a matter of fact - (coyly) I am a
                triplet. Three girls. We were born at one
                thirty in the morning ..... no, no, my sisters
                don't interest themselves in the beauty business
                ..... but of course. We look exactly alike.
                We're triplets. You couldn't tell us apart. I
                don't suppose they'll ever be a time when you
                could tell us apart. (Laughs.)Oh, well, of course,
                if we all live to be a hundred ... yes, it really
                is my ambition ..... forgive me; the heat, the
                lights, I'm so tired ....
                (She collapses into an untidy heap on the table.
                Silence.
                Then ROBERTA gets up. Goes to buffet. Takes
                another canapé. Eats it. As she does so, she
                takes a commemorative telegram from her pock-
                et.   Unfolds it.)

ROBERTA   (Reads aloud.) 'May I take this opportunity of
                congratulating you on the occasion of your one
                hundredth birthday. May you continue to thrive
                and prosper - and during the celebrations of this
                momentous day, do go easy on the cream cakes
                and fizzy lemonade.' (She folds telegram. Puts

it back in her pocket.) How nice. Read yours,
Pauline. What does it say?

PAULINE   What?

ROBERTA   Your telegram from the Queen, dear.

(PAULINE sniffs. Takes telegram from pocket.
Unfolds it.)

PAULINE   (Reads aloud.) 'May I take this opportunity of
congratulating you on the occasion of your one
hundredth birthday. May you continue to thrive
and prosper - and during the celebrations of
this momentous day, do go easy on the cream
cakes and fizzy lemonade. '

(She folds telegram. Puts it back in her
pocket. Pause.)

ROBERTA   Couched in very similar terms. How nice.
Royalty has a way with it. I wonder if Ham's
is different, too. (Moves to table.) Ham,
wake up dear.

(HAM stirs.)

We're reading our telegrams from the Queen.
Do read yours.

(HAM raises herself up. Sits on edge of table.)

HAM   How beautiful am I?

ROBERTA   Very beautiful, Ham.

HAM   You're not just saying that .... ?

ROBERTA   Oh no.

HAM   I always had the feeling you were just that bit more attractive than I.

ROBERTA   Not true.

HAM   I thought there might be a bit of cheapness in
                   my bone structure - round the eyes.

ROBERTA   I'm sure I never noticed. I believe it was
                   remarked at one time, we all had exactly the
                   same bone structure.

HAM   I was told once, many years ago ... I was told
                   once that my forehead was too prominent.

ROBERTA   Never.

HAM   That my chin was weak.

ROBERTA   Never.

HAM   That my lips were too thin.

ROBERTA   Never in a hundred years.

                   (Pause.)

HAM   I do love you, Roberta. (Takes her hands.)
                   There's a sort of majesty in our relationship;
                   yours and mine and Pauline's; nothing will
                   erode it; nothing will assail us; nothing will
                   take from us the beauty and the spirit which
                   inescapably binds us.

                   (Pause.)

ROBERTA   (touched) I believe - yes, I believe those were
                   your last words you spoke to me in eighteen
                   ninety-two. Dear Ham. What did you make of
                   your life?

                   (A pause. HAM then starts to talk. Mouths her
                   story - but no sound at first. ROBERTA nods

and interjects the following occasionally:)

.... You were just a young gel .... No one
could blame you .... Of course, you needed to
find a husband .. Before it was too pronounced
..... No one could blame you for that ...Very
wise ... Very wise .... Dear Ham ..... Was
he really? ....

HAM

(audible) ... Very handsome, and as innocent
as a graveyard. I stepped into a carriage drawn
by two white horses .... the day was balmy,
and I could hear the church bells - distant;
muffled by the shoulder .... muffled by the
weald .... the horses ran, and passing labour-
ers tipped their caps .... the church was near
.... the priest standing in the porch .... he
greeted me as the bells rang out and the sun
shone .... the bells were loud and the sun was
hot, and the priest smiled and patted my veil
and stroked my gloves ... and the organ played
some Bach ... and a tiny linnet fell from its
nest. (Pause.) And we waited .... waited till
the bells were silent; waited till the linnet
died .... waited, waited ... catch me; catch
me; light as a feather; catch me .... into the
vestry ..... lay me down ..... rub my wrists
..... smelling salts, smelling salts ..... pat
me, pet me, help me .... triplet, triplet,
triplet ....

(Pause. HAM is staring at the floor. ROBERTA
backs away. Then HAM rolls over from her
sitting position on to her stomach, and starts
scrabbling to haul herself on to the table as
before. She manages to spreadeagle herself
as before. Then lies still.
ROBERTA goes again to the buffet.   Chooses
another morsel.)

ROBERTA

(to PAULINE) I'll get fat. (Eats.)

PAULINE   Are you rich, Roberta?

ROBERTA   Comfortably off, my dear. It helps to keep up
                   appearances in Windsor. You see, I married a
                   banker. Then I married another banker. And
                   on top of that I married another banker. They
                   made me a lady, a very fine lady with manners
                   and habits. I've been - rubbed up. Now we have
                   become reunited, you must visit me. Bring your
                   husband and children. Ah, but then you've out-
                   lived them all, of course.

PAULINE   Oh no. Charlie's still alive, and the boys.

ROBERTA   How wonderful. That is wonderful. Dear me,
                   I've outlived three husbands, and here you are;
                   your family living on - you living on .... it
                   really is most famous. Do have one of these
                   little things. They're so nice.

                   (Offers plate. PAULINE turns her nose up.)

                   No? (Laughs.) Not enough body for you, mmm,
                   Pauline? Is that it? You like potatoes and dump-
                   lings. (excitedly) Pauline, I'll cook you lots of
                   potatoes and dumplings if you'll visit me with your
                   family. Do come. In the summer. What kind of
                   man is your husband? Does he spit in the fire-
                   place? No matter. Nothing matters. Oh, I know
                   we've drifted, each along our own little road ...
                   we've lost touch, we've lost identity .... all the
                   common ground has gone - but I'm sure, in my
                   little cottage at Windsor we can talk together and
                   laugh together - you and I, your dear husband,
                   and your three sons. Oh do come. Please. What
                   kind of people are your sons? Are they good boys?
                   Do they care for you ?

PAULINE   My husband and my sons don't care for me.

ROBERTA   Really not?

PAULINE   They don't live with me.

ROBERTA   Really not?

PAULINE   They're mad, Roberta. They were all in the
                         wars and they're mad.

                         (A silence. ROBERTA turns away. Momentary
                         half-hearted scrabbling from HAM. Then
                         ROBERTA moves down. Looks up at banner.)

ROBERTA   (quietly) Look what they've done for us. So
                         kind. I think there's too much said about the
                         selfish and the inconsiderate side of people.
                         Not enough is said about the tenderness that can
                         manifest itself - unbidden, unheralded I
                         met a man only yesterday .... he helped me
                         across the road ..... he steered me gently ...
                         I felt his hand on my shoulder .... then on the
                         back of my neck .... he stroked my ear as we
                         crossed.... I felt his thigh pressed against
                         mine .... and I felt the warmth of his caress..
                         he fondled my shoulder-blades.... then - then
                         he tore at my clothing - frenzied, burning ....
                         we, we toppled over onto a Zebra-crossing and
                         rolled against a bollard .... we thrust against
                         each other... he touched me near the traffic-
                         lights .... red, then amber then go .... no ...
                         no parking .... keep left ... no parking .....
                         one way ..... give way ..... give way, give
                         way.... (She staggers to a chair. Sits.)

PAULINE   (tearfully) I want to go home .... I'm an old
                         woman .... too old for this stuff .... too old
                         for this stuff .... I could walk from here. My
                         house is less than a mile. I want to dust my
                         pianos. I want to dust my pianos. And the
                         electricity man is due. He wants to cut me off.
                         He wants to cut me off and duff me up. He wants
                         to smash my teeth in. I've got to be there. I
                         want to be sitting in my rocker. (sobbing) I
                         can't pay. I can't pay. I can't pay. I want to
                         sit in my rocker and go off my rocker. Let me
                         go. Off my rocker .... too old ... too old. I'm

dismal. Dismal.

ROBERTA   (chirpy) God was in Harrods last week. He
                       was buying some silk socks. He asked me if
                       they wore well. I told Him my third husband
                       swore by them. (Pause.) He used a Barclay
                       card. God used a Barclay card. He came
                       right out with it. He waved it around to show
                       everybody He meant business. (forcefully)
                       You just cannot trifle with Him when He's in
                       that mood.

                       (Pause. HAM sits up.)

                       Hello Ham. Read your telegram.

HAM   (Giggles and sings to the tune:'Hello, Hello,
                       who's your lady-friend?')
                       Hello-Ham, Hello-Ham, Read your Telegram..
                       .... (Laughs.) Hello-Ham, Hello-Ham, read
                       your Telegram....(Laughs.)

ROBERTA   (with all naturalness) Get on with it. Stop
                       taking the piss.

                       (HAM chuckles, searches for telegram. Finds
                       it. Opens it.)

HAM   (Reading it.) 'May I take this opportunity of
                       congratulating you on the occasion of your one
                       hundredth birthday, you old bag. May you
                       continue to be a drain and a drag on society -
                       and during the celebrations of this momentous
                       day, may you drop dead from over eating.'
                       (HAM giggles.)

ROBERTA   How true. How true that is. Have we not
                       aged petulantly - like children? Age really
                       does degrade the skin and bone of humanity;
                       it really does lower the tone of God's beautiful
                       design. (Pause.) We're treated far too well.
                       Look what they've done for us ...

HAM (as if giving an interview) The pity of it is, you see, sir, I'm a triplet. Oh yes, just one. I'm only one triplet. I'm not a complete triple. Oh no. Not complete. I'm just a third. I'm not a Trinity. No, no, no, not even a Holy Trinity. Just a triplet. A nice triplet? Well, thank you. I've always lived under the misapprehension that I lacked. Yes, lacked. That I wasn't the prettiest like the other two are the prettiest. Oh yes, the other two are the prettiest, sir. Oh yes, we're identical. We're more than identical, sir. We're the same. But the other two are prettier. Now that's a good question, sir. How - penetrating you can be. I like a man with penetration. That is indeed a good question to put to an innocent girl.... Will we always be identical? ..... how penetrating. (Pause.) What on earth could Life do to us that would make us otherwise?

(HAM falls back on the table, and is racked with low animal groans. She writhes and threshes, and emits high-pitched squeals. She grows still and silent. Then she sits up, and carries on talking to 'interviewer' as if nothing had happened.)

Well, I shall spend some of my prize money on a bicycle made for three.

(Pause. All three are staring into space. When they next speak they are children. They do not act out the situations with any form of movement. They sit quite still.)

ROBERTA Flashings, dada .... don't like them .....

PAULINE No, no ... don't like them, take them away ...

ROBERTA Smokings and flashings, dada .... take them away .....

PAULINE	Nasty lights ...
ROBERTA	Nasty people ... take them away ...
HAM	Firesticks, mama .... mama....
ROBERTA	Nasty monster .... dada....
PAULINE	Nasty monster ..... please,dada ....
ROBERTA	Dada, take it away ....
HAM	Three .... three .... three ....
ROBERTA	Please, take it away ....
PAULINE	Smoke .... smoke ....
HAM	Three. Legs. Three. Legs. (Screams.)
ROBERTA	Dada ... dada... flashings, dada .. (Screams.)
PAULINE	Toggaphy ... toggaphy ... don't like toggaphy. (Screams.)

(All three start to cry in that heartrending manner of all small children - starting high, going down on a short curve - pausing for breath, then starting high again.
They are synchronised in their sobbing. They bawl and bawl. Then stop abruptly - together. They sit with their mouths open.
Pause.
They are still children through following.)

ROBERTA	(quietly) Don't want ta go ... won't go in ... no mama....
PAULINE	(sniffling) Nasty old man on the door ... on the door.....
ROBERTA	On the door ..... we shan't ....

HAM   The band is loud, mama ... it hurts my ears ...

PAULINE   Hurts my ears ....

ROBERTA   Won't dress up. Shan't.

PAULINE   Shan't....

HAM   Shan't....

PAULINE   It's hot .... help ....

HAM   The drums are loud.... leave us alone ...

ROBERTA   The people are packed .. they're packed ...

PAULINE   Packed .... let me go home ...

HAM   They clap ... they laugh ...

ROBERTA   Leave us alone ....

PAULINE   Let me go home ....

HAM   Leave us alone ....

PAULINE   Let me go home ....

               (They are all snivelling.)

HAM   Don't want to dance ....

ROBERTA   No ... no ... shan't sing a song ...

HAM   Shan't dance ... shan't smile ...

ROBERTA   Will say shan't ...

HAM   Shan't stop saying shan't ...

ROBERTA   Shan't ....

HAM	Shan't ...
ROBERTA	Shan't ...
HAM	Shan't, shan't, shan't, shan't....
ROBERTA	Shan't, shan't, shan't, shan't ...
	(They peter out. Pause.)
PAULINE	(normal voice) Let me go home ...
	(HAM falls back on table. Lies prone.)
ROBERTA	(normal voice) I remember ... I remember we made a pact. (Gets up.) Yes, we made a pact. Can you recall our pact, Pauline?
PAULINE	Let me go home ....
ROBERTA	We were – how old were we? Sixteen? I think we were sixteen. We sat together in the garden. I recall the sound of father's cello, drifting out to us... how marvellous it all was ... and we made a pact. We vowed that we would – separate. We wouldn't give the world the opportunity to – to plague us. (Pause.) I think we stuck to it pretty well. (She moves to HAM. Leans over her.) Dear Ham. Poor Ham. I think we stuck to it pretty well. (Strokes HAM. HAM stirs, then lies still. ROBERTA moves away, chattering.) I was talking to God last Tuesday morning; we were talking about this and that, and I said: tell me, why did You make us identical? It was quite a feat. Why did You make us similar? Why did You multiply me by three? (Pause.) And God replied: I'm a bit of a show-off.

PAULINE

We should stay apart, Roberta. We move in different circles. We're different. We're different.

ROBERTA

(thoughtfully) We're not the same ...

PAULINE

We're different. At last. (Pause.) Things frighten me .... so many things frighten me. You're not like that, Roberta. Nothing frightens you.

ROBERTA

Oh, but it does.

PAULINE

You've never been frightened.

ROBERTA

Oh, but I have. In fact, quite recently, I was very frightened, Pauline. Terribly so. I saw a man and his wife - a very devoted couple I might add; neighbours of mine - I saw them eat their children. They had three: all girls. They went out into the garden, scooped them up, and ate them without any preparation or dressing. Then they sat on the lawn: bloated and bloody - and cried and cried and cried. It was then that they frightened me. What they did next shook me to the core. I'll never forget it if I live to be - if I live to be ....

(ROBERTA puts her face in her hands. HAM sits up suddenly. Hands on hips.)

HAM

(talking to someone imaginary) I've had more lovers than you've had hot dinners. What? What? ... get on with yer. During my years as a beauty queen? Chaperoned? What? (Laughs.) Now look, lay off. I know the score. Keep off. Stop - touching me. I make the choice. I've always been beautiful and I can make the choices. I've chosen this one and that one - any time, any place. So keep off, don't touch. Wait till I give the word. When I give

the word I'll be alluring .... yes, I'll switch
on the magnetism, I'll give you a quick flash.
So watch it. Watch for the signal. (angered)
Look, I said don't touch, mister. Get off ....
(She is sitting on front edge of table. During
following she backslides her way up to back
edge of table.) Leave me ... you dirty - you
dirty ... off. Off. Off. I haven't given you
leave ... (Screams.)... I'll have you for that.
Look what you've just done, you - you bestial..
... off me, off me ... (She is at top edge.) Do
you know who I am? I'll tell you. I'm - I'm -
(The anger goes. Small voice. Fear.)   ....
... Mister, mister, please - please, mister ...
I'm a triplet ... (small child/old woman sob)
... triplet, triplet, triplet .... (She continues
intoning 'triplet' through following:)

PAULINE

I'm frightened. Let me go home. I'm frightened.... frightened .... frightened...........
(PAULINE continues to intone 'frightened'
through following:)

ROBERTA

... If I live to be a hundred. What they did next
made my blood run cold ... made me feel ash-
amed ... and futile ... and at odds with all
humankind ... they - they began to weed the
garden. That's what they did. They pulled up
handfuls of suckers by the scruff of the neck.
Poor little plants. Poor little suckers ...poor
little suckers ... poor little suckers ...

(All three intone their last spoken words.
PAULINE and ROBERTA wander aimlessly.
HAM is cowering on the table-top.
In a moment THE MAYORESS enters. She is a
large woman, wearing her chain of office and a
fashionable hat and suit. The moment she enters
the three old ladies stop talking, but they continue to snivel.)

MAYORESS

(to HAM) What are you doing on the table? Get

down at once. (to the others) Now, are you
tidy? Let me look at you.

(HAM slides off table. Stands sulking.)

The Queen's outside - she's just outside, and
she's in a foul temper. She stepped out of her
limousine straight into a puddle, and her feet
are soaking wet. (Bristling) And all the town
clerk could do was stand there with his coat on.
Now, let's have you. What's this? Tears?
(Looks at HAM.) Tears? Oh, that will never do.
Come now. Stand just here. Line up just here.
Let's make sure you're tidy.

(The old ladies are assembled and jostled into
a position for presentation.)

My word. You've given us a lot of trouble and no
mistake. I'll be glad when the week's over.
Yarmouth and Windsor have been giving us no end
of trouble. But we won the day. Oh yes, we won
the day. The fact that you were all born here
clinched it. We weren't going to let some other
snotty borough have all the gravy. Oh no. This
is a wonderful opportunity to put us all on the map
again. We haven't been on the map since that
multiple rape case in '62.

(She has been fussing them during this - adjusting
ribbons and frocks.)

Now. Let's see. Hmm. (Looks closely at
ROBERTA.) You've got crumbs round your mouth.
Naughty. (Takes handkerchief from her pocket,
wets the corner with saliva and administers to
ROBERTA.) Now, I told you not to touch that
buffet. I made a point of stressing that. Those
little delicacies are very modish, and besides
the Council haven't paid for it yet. There we are.
(Stands back.) Now remember what I said about

curtsying. Front knee bend, other leg stretched
rearwards and crossed. And for Heaven's sake
keep your balance. The Queen will not be amu-
sed if you collapse in an untidy heap. Besides,
there's no excuse for it. Right? Good. (Moves
to door.) Now, no more silly tears. This is
your big day. The band is on the Town Hall
steps, ready to strike up. There's a tin-box
collection going on amongst the crowd, in aid of
retired councillors; a lot of townspeople have
turned out to see you. We've manufactured little
plastic triplet-badges for distribution around all
the schools; and one boutique in the High Street
is selling triplet T-shirts and Y-fronts. And
the editor of our local newspaper has been run-
ning a triplet competition all this month in con-
junction with the Family Planning Clinic. Now.
  (pause) Brace yourselves, my loves. This is
your big day.

(She exits, leaving door open.
A pause.
The triplets stand quite still.
Off stage, distant, a brass band plays 'Happy
Birthday'. It stops.
Pause.
Then PAULINE starts to snivel.
ROBERTA looks at her.
PAULINE stops.
Then HAM moves to conference table, and
attempts to clamber on to it as at beginning.
She breathes in and out deeply and noisily.
ROBERTA looks at her.
Ham gets on to table - and stands, still breathing
like an animal.
She poses, beauty queen-fashion, still breathing
like an animal.
The noise she makes grows.
Then, frenzied, she tears at her wig and mask.
She is unable to remove either at first. Then,
in the throes of some turmoil, HAM tears the
wig and mask off.

She is instantly calm and at peace.
She has the face of a young, cheeky-looking girl.
She smiles.
A pause.)

HAM   (tiny voice) Trip ..... let.